Blackout Poetry Journal
Poetic Therapy #2

© 2018 Kathryn Maloney

Step 1: Underline or circle the perfect words or phrases for you poem or hidden message.

Step 2: Blackout (or use your artistic ability) to hide everything else.

Step 3: Read and share!

Take a picture and share on your favorite social media site!

Share it on Kathryn Maloney's Facebook Author's Page!

www.facebook.com/kimaloney

Google Blackout Poetry to find hundreds of great examples to get your creative spirit.

Find Kathryn's Blackout Poetry examples at:

www.kimaloney.com

THE THREE APPLES.

"Why, my dear," said his mother, "I mean that when we lack anything this world can give, we must fetch the more from heaven."

"You love heaven very much, don't you, mother?" said Mark, looking up at her quite wonderingly.

"More than you love me."

Mark thought that was hardly possible; but he did not like to contradict his mother, and besides, they were now at the church door, and had to go in and take their seats. Mark thought the clergyman chose the strangest text that could be for Thanksgiving Day, it was this:—

"There is nothing at all, beside this manna, before our eyes."

When church was over, and Mark and his mother were walking home again, they were overtaken by little Tom Crab.

"Come," said little Tom, "let us go and sit on the fence and eat apples. We shan't have dinner to-day till ever so late, because it takes so long to get it ready; and I am so hungry. What are you going to have for dinner?"

"I don't know," said Mark.

"I know what we are going to have," said Tom, "only I can't remember everything. It makes me worse than ever to think of it. Come—let us go and eat apples."

"I have not got any," said Mark.

"Haven't got any!" said Tom, dropping Mark's elbow and staring at him—for the idea of a boy without apples had never before occurred to any of Mr. Crab's family. "Oh, you mean you have eaten up all you had in your pocket?"

"No," said Mark, "we haven't had any this year. Last year Mr. Smith gave us a basketful."

"Well, come along, and I'll give you some," said Tom. "I've got six, and I think three will do for me till dinner. "Oh, Mark! you ought to see the goose roasting in our kitchen? I'll tell you what—I think I may as well give you the whole six, because I can run home and get some more; and I might as well be at home,

Sometimes a child, looking out of window into the growing darkness, saw her for a minute, like a wavering moonbeam, and called to the people in the room to hurry to the window, but she had gone before they could get there.

At last she came to a cottage where a cruel mother was beating her little boy. At such a dreadful sight the Spirit began to weep, for the first time in her existence. She felt cold and desolate, but as her tears fell the cruel mother, suddenly ashamed, stayed her hand and allowed the screaming child to drag himself away. He rushed to the door and out into the windy night.

The Spirit stooped down and he ran, blindly, right into her arms. She soothed his cries and laid her hands on his bursting heart, charming it into quietude. Then she led him, fearfully and reluctantly, back into the cottage. He clung to her, sobbing.

She spoke to the mother, who fell back in amazement, white and trembling, staring at her. Then the mother made the sign of the Cross upon her breast.

There were other children in the room, hiding, but as the Lost Spirit crossed the threshold they began to creep out—two from behind the rough wooden press, one from beneath the bed, one from the dark recess by the window. The whimpering of a tiny baby ceased. All eyes were turned upon the Spirit. The flames leapt up upon the hearth to greet her. A great bough of pine in a corner of the room bowed down before her. Even the old oil lamp glowed more brightly, spluttering a little in its excitement.

She gathered the children into her arms, and looked at the overworked mother with tender interest. Then she sat down on the wooden bench by the side of the hearth. Her long, pale hair rippled on the ground.

Presently the man came home. He kicked open the door, and his great dog—half wolf, half dog—sprang in, shaking the snow from his rough coat. He lowered his head at the stranger, and the man behind him, almost as savage and wild as the dog, looked at her in blank astonishment.

The wife was frightened, and the children huddled together like little animals.

Suddenly the man's face changed. An unusual smile

adjusted, when he hit one leg of the stand with his foot and sent the whole into the Basin. In trying to save it, he slipped, and fell in himself. I was standing near him, and, knowing that he could not swim, I made such haste to catch him that I, too, went headlong into the water. The water was icy cold, it being near November. Being a good swimmer, I soon placed my companion where he could hold on for a few minutes, and having got out myself, I helped him to do the same. We were in a bad way, certainly; both of us wet to the skin, and the apparatus fifteen feet under water. The poor fellow actually wept, believing he had lost it forever; but I told him I would get it again, even if I had to dive for it. Procuring a long pole, we made a very good grappling with some nails we had with us, and let it down, but found it too short. Splicing it with cords, we again let it down, and, as I was feeling about for the object of our search, I lost my balance and fell into the Basin a second time. I had, at previous times, like many others, stood on the brink of the Basin, and longed for a plunge in the " delicious-looking bath"; but I changed my mind entirely after this second experience, and at all subsequent visits to the spot, I " looked but longed no more." Undaunted, I climbed out, and we renewed our attempts to recover the apparatus, which we finally succeeded in doing.

Oh! how we capered and laughed, forgetting that we were thoroughly wet, two miles from any house, and without the means to make a fire. By the time that we began to realize our situation, and consider what we should do, a team happened along and we procured some matches of the driver, and determined to stay all night, as we had at first intended. We built a large fire, and so far dried our clothes that we felt comfortable, and then worked on till near sundown, when we looked about for a place to spend the night. I remembered having seen a small shanty, somewhere in the vicinity, a year before, and went to look for it. After a diligent search, I found it about half a mile away, and returned to guide my comrade to it, marking the trees as I went, to insure a speedy return. It was the best place we could find; and we proceeded to make ourselves comfortable, although the fact that there was an old bear-trap near by, brought up rather unpleasant associations; the idea of one of those animals coming along, not being agreeable.

We ate our supper cold, and made our bed with moss and blankets. We were afraid to build a fire in that place, for fear of a conflagration in the woods, a thing which had happened before from the same cause. The gloom of the forest, and the rapidly-increasing darkness, were indeed thrilling. The darkness put it out of our power to converse, which was rather uncomfortable. All was utter silence to me; my companion doing the hearing for both of us, while, I suppose, I did my share of the thinking. Neither of us slept much that night, the strangeness of my position and my own thoughts keeping me awake; while the

THE QUEEN OF THE PIRATE ISLE.

This last infamous suggestion fired the corsair's blood. "Dy'ar think we daresent," said Hickory, desperately, but with an uneasy glance at Polly. "I'll show yer to-morrow."

The entrance of Polly's mother at this moment put an end to Polly's authority and dispersed the pirate band, but left Wan Lee's proposal and Hickory's rash acceptance ringing in the ears of the Pirate Queen. That evening she was unusually silent. She would have taken Bridget, her nurse, into her confidence, but this would have involved a long explanation of her own feelings, from which, like all imaginative children, she shrank. She, however, made preparation for the proposed flight by settling in her mind which of her two dolls she would take. A wooden creature with easy going knees and moveable hair seemed to be more fit for hard service and any indiscriminate scalping that might turn up hereafter. At supper, she timidly asked a question of Bridget. "Did ye ever hear the loikes uv that, Ma'am," said the Irish handmaid with affectionate pride. "Shure the darlint's head

aware, as winter changes the trees. My love for Heathcliff resembles the eternal rocks beneath: a source of little visible delight, but necessary. Nelly, I *am* Heathcliff! He's always, always in my mind: not as a pleasure, any more than I am always a pleasure to myself, but as my own being." (Chapter 9)

At the deepest level, psychic decomposition may be part of the novelist's vision of the world; I agree with Mrs. Van Ghent that this is so with *Great Expectations*. It also seems to me true of *Moby Dick*; the crew of the Pequod may be regarded collectively as Melville's view of the total range of man's possibilities when faced with the voyage of his destiny. In particular, as Leslie Fiedler and other critics have pointed out, the role of Ishmael may be seen as a dramatization of Melville's simultaneous complicity in, and detachment from, what he took to be a diabolic vision; the narrative structure of the book, as it fluctuates between epic and dramatic modes of presentation, thus being the formal correlative of theme. Again, do we not feel that the Karamazov family exist in a single psychological or spiritual continuum, so that without detracting from their individuality or without straying into allegory, Dostoievski is saying something not just about men—Aloysha, Ivan, Dmitri—but also about Man?

We must retreat from such clouded and speculative depths; the problem is, of its nature, one destroyed by the light of logical analysis.

> Tragedy, [Yeats wrote] must always be a drowning and breaking of the dykes that separate man from man, and ... it is upon those dykes that comedy keeps house ... behind the momentary self, which acts and lives in the world, and is subject to the judgement of the world, there is that which cannot be called before any mortal judgement seat.... We may not find either mood in its purity, but in mainly tragic art one distinguishes devices to exclude or lessen character, to diminish the power of that daily mood, to cheat or blind its too clear perception.[1]

Asylum, and for the welfare of the generous instructors and founders.

At the Suspension Bridge we took the cars for Portage, passing, on our road, Perry, Wyoming and several other little villages. When we left the cars and took a carriage, our way lay along a high ridge of hills. The carriage track was very narrow, with scarcely a foot space between it and a frightful precipice on one side, and a high, steep bank on the other. I trembled and clung to the side of the carriage, fearing every moment to be dashed to destruction—a single mis-step of the horses, or mismanagement on the part of the the driver, making such a result inevitable. But we passed over safely. Every now and then entering some densely wooded dingle or tangled wild, which made it seem as if we were hundreds of miles from any human habitation, and then a sudden turn in the road would reveal the most enchanting little village imaginable, nestled in a warm valley at our feet; we could look directly down upon the roofs of some of them. It seemed to me like fairy land. Thus we were several times surprised and delighted during our ride.

The Portage Falls, though much smaller than the Niagara, looked very beautiful, flying and flashing in the sunlight, and pouring its sheet of white foam down the rocks.

Messenger's Hollow was another beautiful town, situated at the foot of the Alleghany Mountains. Indeed, I could fill a large book, describing what I saw through that country, but I can only briefly allude to them here. All along this delightful tour I found much pleasure in conversing with some of

a caries of this portion of the temporal bone, the liquids that were injected, passed down through the Eustachian tube into the back part of the mouth. Dr. Jasser, a Swedish Physician, about the middle of the last century, had a similar case, and, finding that the patient obtained his hearing on one side, he made an opening by means of a trocar, and produced the same effect on the other side. With the exception of this person, it has never proved successful: there have been many attempts made to afford relief by this method, every one of which produced very distressing, and dangerous symptoms. I have not been able to trace, whether it has, or has not, been performed in England; but I have heard from many patients, that they have been solicited by country surgeons to al-

would no longer keep out the wet. The little maid was delighted at the thought of a new dress; for her Sunday one was almost up to her knees, and there was nothing with which to lengthen it.

Every day she and her brother had looked out for the promised visit from the gentlefolk, but to their disappointment they never came. Tamsin was also disappointed, for she believed that Lady Staversworth was not one to make a promise and not fulfil it. But she heard in her travels to and from St Ives that Howard had been suffering from a feverish cold, and that his mother was far from well. But as she also heard that they drove often to St Ives, she came to the conclusion that her ladyship had forgotten her.

When June was half through, Blaze seemed to suffer less, and his grandmother hoped he would soon pick up strength again, and she set out for Penzance one Tuesday morning with a light heart. But she returned with a heavy one. She had not been able to sell any of her brooms and rush-mats. Added to that, and one or two other worries—small in themselves, but great to her, from the very fact of her poverty—as she was coming through Zennor Churchtown on her way home, somebody told her that it was little Lady Marjorie's birthday on Friday, and that Lady Staversworth was going to honour it by a tea on the cliffs, to which everybody in the parish had been invited.

"Of course, Tamsin, *you and your grandchildren* were the first to be asked," said the woman in conclusion, "for we were told that their ladyships have drank tea in your cottage."

"It is the first time I have heard anything about the little lady's birthday," returned Tamsin.

"Well, to be sure!" ejaculated the woman; "why, Parson was sent to ask my man, little maid, and me, two days ago. You must have offended them somehow, Tamsin. Gentry are terrible touchy, I've heard folks say, and that if you only step 'pon their toes 'tis all up with you in the way of favours."

CHAPTER IX.

As Willy would not pay the extra fare, Frank had to travel second class. Willy was telling his friend of the Stock Exchange, and how he had lost nearly four thousand pounds. He had suspected that the firm of which he was junior partner had not played fair with him. Anyhow, he was going to get out of the business. He had something else in view—a shop in Brighton. Yes, a shop in Brighton, a greengrocer's shop. No one had any idea, until they went into the calculation, of the amount of profit that was made on vegetables. Lord This and Lord That, everyone who had a handsome place with large gardens, counted on being able to pay his gardener's wages by the sale of the surplus carrots, artichokes, potatoes, parsley, onions, tomatoes, especially tomatoes—every one nowadays ate tomatoes. He had it all down in figures, and was perfectly astonished at the sums of money that could be made. Grapes had been overdone, that was true; but a profit could be made out of everything else. Flowers, especially gardenias, were sold in the London market at two shillings apiece. Now, there was he within five miles of a large town like Brighton; the rent of a shop in the Western Road would not come to more than seventy or eighty pounds a year; the missus he would put in as shopwoman, and he would guarantee that she would make as good a shopwoman as you could find, after a little practice; the child could run on errands,

On Illumination.

may be but indifferent artifts in general defign, and with a great deal of fuccefs, whilft others converfant with the higheft principles of art have frequently been found to be but very indifferent illuminators. The reafon of this is obvious; illuminating being for the moft part a ftrictly mechanical art (though fubject to artiftical principles), any one gifted with natural abilities, tafte, patience and perfeverance, will by ftudioufly following out fome flight mechanical contrivance, eafily attain the firft principles primarily neceffary to copy any given outline however intricate; not even excluding the human figure. The ornamental arabefque fcroll from its primitive fimplicity to the moft elaborate finifhed foliage, interlaced initials, etc., are next given in due fucceffion for the pupil to copy; by which means his hand is gradually trained to curval delineations, his hand and eye gets gradually educated, till at laft all angular tendency in his ornamentations becomes entirely eradicated; once trained to that perfection, colouring and fhading becomes comparatively trivial, and a little inftruction with a trifling felf practice will enable the uneducated artift to overcome almoft every obftacle. The artift, on the other hand, relying on his capacity alone, and difregarding the contrivance given at his command, not unfrequently ftumbles over the eafieft parts, pettifhly condemns all me-

KNIGHTS FIGHTING.
BRAVE AND TRUE.

end of the knife to keep the onion-juice from making her cry, and asked her to make him a small basin of paste, her kitchen majesty uttered a loud snort.

"Which I just shan't," she cried; "and if your Mar was at home you wouldn't dare to ask. I never did see such a tiresome, worriting boy as you are, Master Ned. You're always wanting something when I'm busy; and what your master's a-thinking about to give you such long holidays at midsummer I don't know."

"They aren't long," said Ned, indignant at the idea of holidays being too long for a boy of eleven.

"Don't you contradict, sir, or I'll just tell your Mar; and the sooner you're out of my kitchen the better for you. Be off, both of you!"

It was on Tizzy's little red lips to say: "Oh, please do make some paste!" but she was not peeling onions, and had no knife with a piece of bread-crumb at the end to keep the tears from coming. So come they did, and sobs with them to stop the words.

"Never mind, Tiz," cried Ned, lifting her on to a chair. "Here, get on my back and I'll carry you. Cook's in a tantrum this morning."

Tizzy placed her arms round her brother's neck and clung tightly while he played the restive steed, and raised Cook's ire to redhot-point by purposely kicking one of the Windsor chairs, making it scroop on the beautifully-white floor of the front kitchen, and making the queen of the domain rush out at him, looking red-eyed and ferocious, for the onion-juice had affected her.

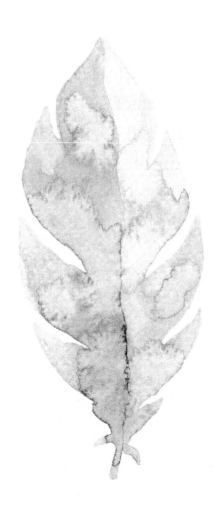

quieted down to my normal state, when I recalled with bitterness and renewed longing, the eternal uniform music of the ocean and how sublime it was in its immeasureableness.

The lighthouse, though built on the edge of a steep, surf bound rock, was hardly that ideal place sentimental authors have kindly foisted upon us. There was no black isolation about it. A village with hideous polychromatic summer cottages, reflecting in their silly architecture the anarchism of our age, was within a mile's reach.

The keeper of the lighthouse was a taciturn old fellow, short and sturdy, a phlegmatic, self-reliant nature who could get well along without people, satisfied with smoking his pipe and growling to himself while polishing the brass of his lanterns. The bottle of Kentucky Bourbon, which I always managed to bring with me, however, made him more accessible. His wife, bred in the paltry but self-satisfied comfort of the middle classes, was one of those creatures who can not get accustomed to new ways, thus she longed for the days when she went shopping in her native town, promenaded on the avenues with a wasp waist and spotted tulle veil, and drove out on Sundays with her best young man. Now she had to bring up "her brats," and the isolation of her curious little home and paralian existence seemed to weigh upon her commonplace character.

On one of these visits towards the end of the year, the idea struck me that it would be quite a novel experience to arrange a genuine German Christmas Eve in the lighthouse, and I promised the lighthousekeeper's wife and children to show up when Christmas came, however lack of funds prevented me; the following year the stormy weather made the trip impossible. At last, after two years of postponement, I arrived toward dusk, with a Christmas tree, boxes of candles, and candies, and a few other insignificant presents in my boat. The old keeper recognized me at once and grinned as I shook my bottle of Bourbon whiskey at him. His wife greeted me cordially: "I am glad that you have come, it would have otherwise been so lonely here to-night."

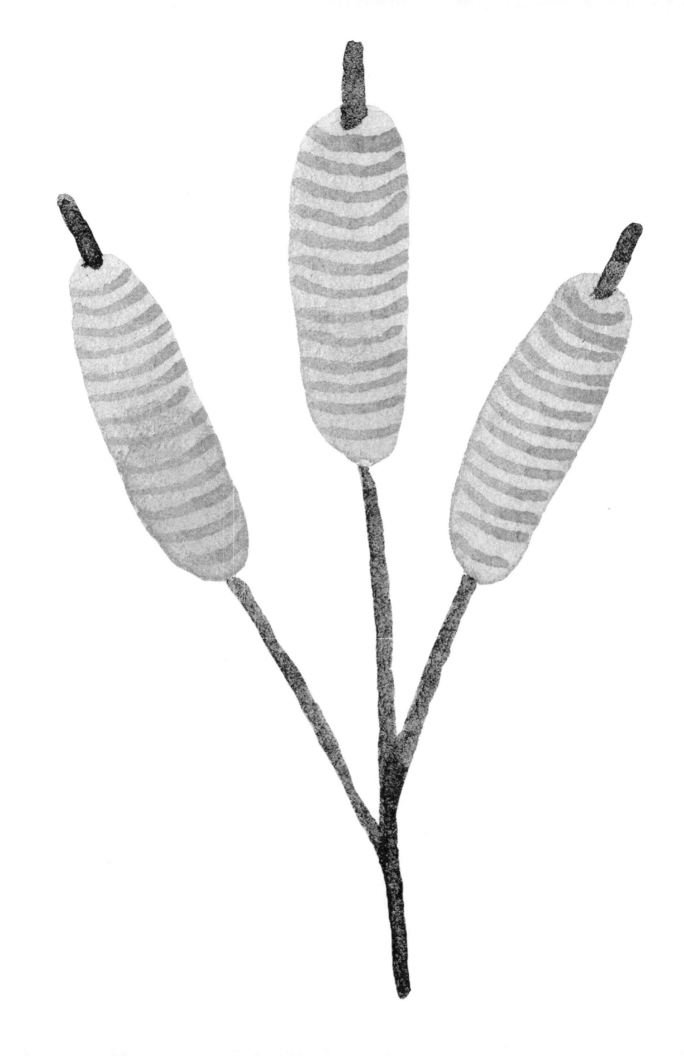

AN EXPENSIVE LUXURY.

that was at a presidential election soon after reaching our majority. We voted for ——, but no matter. To offend party prejudice at this time might be fatal to our hopes. The day after the election we received a bill of two dollars for "poll-tax," which the collector said we owed and we had better pay or have our body lodged in the county jail until we should call for it, and settle up what was due on it to the State. The unprincipled man had obtained our address from the registry books, and this our first ebulition of patriotism cost us two dollars.

However much inclined we may be by nature and experience to avoid the subject of politics as a rule, it now becomes our duty to make mention of certain exponents of American politics, but whether to their ad-

The Seventeenth-century song-writers were plain spoken, and they loved pleasure, but they were not corrupt; there was too much vitality in them. The love of women, which had inexhaustible attraction for them, and which they have clothed in all manner of charms, is distinctly concrete in the simplicity and frankness with which it exalts beauty of face and form, but it does not rest in any kind of visible loveliness; there is a touch of chivalry, of romance, of exaltation, of mysticism in it. It is frank and often sensuous, but the note of morbid passion, of diseased emotion, is absent. It is far more healthful than a great deal of verse which is more guarded in expression, because it is natural, and it is, for the most part, innocent. These old poets had a wholesome love of the beauty of life, and it must be frankly said of them, that their dealing with certain forms of that beauty was far more healthful than the manner and attitude of some of their Puritan successors. They felt the rich loveliness of the world, but they knew also that it was fleeting. It was Herrick, whose hand was sometimes far too free, who said:

Howard;" and with that rush, usually seen when some old "bell weather" takes the lead, the fashion and the *élite*, snobs, nobs, patrician and *parvenue*, made one unanimous, double grand and essential stampede *there;* and the house was not only filled, night after night, to utter suffocation, but tickets commanded a premium unknown since the days of the immortal Kean, and the high-hopping queen of ——, Fanny Ellsler, raising the safety-valve of the treasury to a high concert, and most devoutly wished-for pitch.

It will be perceived that at this period we had four theatres open, and, in a moderate degree, very successful; whereas, but a little twelvemonth before, we had but one; and even that, if we believe the assertions of the "dead-heads," was on the rapid decline, but for their succor and support. (!) Previous to this great dramatic revolution, actors were plentier and cheaper than Cremona performers in Pluto's cuisine, but now, bless ye! they invoiced their services at the most exorbitant terms, and each actor, arrayed in a suit of *real* clothes, fresh from the shelves of *Oak Hall*, grew ever so "pot-gutted," and "put on airs" that fairly knocked the dust from the heels of the managers; and many bar-rooms and bowling-alleys, that had long threatened their proprietors with pecuniary strangulation, now bid fair to loom up and flourish, like unto ye green bay horse!

Previous to the *debut* of the "Very Nice Children," the "Baron" had secured and retained (about the only retainers his baronial estate ever did retain) a very good company, although a very bad working one, as they signally failed to keep the house clear of the "dead wood" of expenses. Now it was mistrusted that the "Baron" had some funds, stowed away, while nobody ever began to suspect, that the "Doctor" had the first *red*. The Baron did not expect, and further was it from his *intention*, than Pluto's remotest region from the gates of Paradise, that *he* should then and there play a *losing* game; inasmuch, as before the lapse of eight consecutive weeks the Baron gave out unmistakable signs to — vamose, take the Sabine slide, or whatever else you, gentle reader, may be pleased to *call — cutting one's lucky!*

But somebody says, which of the poets we do not dis-

THE STORY OF PETER PAN

taken up to the now desolate nursery, where Mrs. Darling spent most of her time mourning for her lost children, while the faithful Nana tried in vain to cheer her up. "George, George, I believe you are beginning to *like* that kennel," she said reproachfully as he crawled out. He denied the charge however, and tried to comfort Mrs. Darling, who never for one moment forgot the little empty beds and the silence and cheerlessness of the nursery. Then he left her, and sitting down by the fire, Mrs. Darling was alone with her sad thoughts.

Scarcely however had she closed her eyes when three little figures flew in at the window and nestled cosily in their beds. Then softly Wendy called to her mother. But when Mrs. Darling looked round she simply couldn't believe that the children were really there. So many times before she had dreamt of their return, that it was not till they all three crowded round her that she realized that they had indeed come home. Oh! what joy to feel once more those dear faces cool and fresh from the flight through the night air pressed against hers, hot with tears; to hear once more the sound of those sweet voices as they all talked at once. At last, when she was a little calm, Wendy began telling her about

and takes its place on the bottom rank of the Princeton host opposite. Terrific cheers from the enemy.

Another crash of music, and from our end of the horseshoe comes the Harvard band, with its tail of undergrads, to face the enemy across the greensward. Terrific cheers from ourselves.

The fateful hour is imminent. It is time to unleash the dogs of war. Three flannelled figures leap out in front of the Princeton host. They shout through megaphones to the enemy. They rush up and down the line, they wave their arms furiously in time, they leap into the air. And with that leap there bursts from twenty thousand throats a barbaric chorus of cheers roared in unison and in perfect time, shot through with strange, demoniacal yells, and culminating in a gigantic bass growl, like that of a tiger, twenty thousand tigers leaping on their prey—the growl rising to a terrific snarl that rends the heavens.

The glove is thrown down. We take it up. We send back yell for yell, roar for roar. Three cheer-leaders leap out on the greensward in front of us, and to their screams of command and to the wild gyrations of their limbs we stand up and shout the battle-cry of Harvard. What it is like I cannot hear, for I am lost in its roar. Then the band opposite leads off with the battle-song of Princeton, and, thrown out by twenty thousand lusty pairs of lungs, it hits us like a Niagara of sound. But, unafraid, we rise like one man and, led by our band and kept in time by our cheer-leaders, gesticulating before us on the greensward like mad dervishes, we shout back the song of " Har-vard ! Har-vard ! "

her eyes against his and swayed away from him to the cold window-pane.

"I see," she whispered, "you don't want me—you couldn't—*you—never—did!*"

And at that instant the blood bond in Andrew Sevier's breast snapped and with an awed comprehension of the vast and everlasting Source from which flows the love that constrains and the love that heals, the love that only comes to bind in honor, he reached out and took his own. In the seventh heaven which is the soul haunt of all in like case, there was no need of word mating.

Hours later, one by one the lights in the houses along the avenue twinkled out and the street lay in the grasp of the after midnight silence. Only a bright light still burned at the major's table, which was piled high with books into which he was delving with the hunger of many long

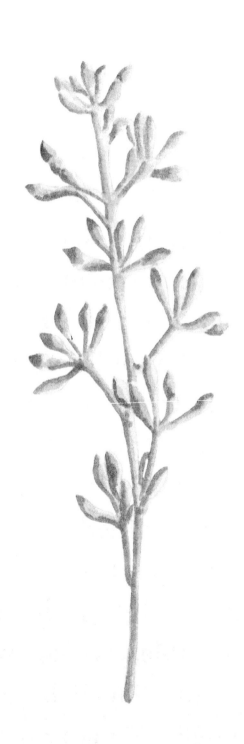

gether was merely a convenience; the moral significance touched neither her heart nor her mind. In her the primordial craving for ease, for material comforts, pretty trinkets and gowns was strongest developed. It was as if this sense had been handed down to her, untouched by contact with progression, from the remote ages, that time between the fall of Roman civilization and where modern civilization began. In short, a beautiful barbarian, whose intellect alone had advanced.

Fortune was asleep. The mother went over to the bed and gently shook the slim, round arm which lay upon the coverlet. The child's nature lay revealed as she opened her eyes and smiled. It did not matter that the smile instantly changed to a frowning inquiry. The mother spoke truly when she said that there were times when she stood in awe of this, her flesh and blood.

"My child, I wish to ask you a question, and for your own good answer truthfully. Do you love Horace?"

Fortune sat up and rubbed her eyes. "No." Had her wits been less scattered she might have paltered.

The syllable had a finality to it that reassured the

THE CHALLENGE

and at last, without plan, made virtue of his necessity and went boldly across the room.

Still she did not move, but stood looking at him with the same expression of passive expectancy and waited for him to come. His mind refused to work with any clearness and, when he was close to her, he was simply conscious that he had taken the hand she offered and was murmuring to her some form of inarticulate speech.

There did not for the moment seem the need for greeting more distinct, and half-unconsciously his mind employed itself with the impression of her that came to him through his eyes. She was different from what he remembered her to be as he had seen her last, and yet so like, that he was puzzled to determine quite wherein the difference lay.

Her figure was less girlish, as Motrya had said, and she arranged her hair now in a different way. But he decided that the thing that counted was the unremembered expression of her eyes. They were larger somehow and more grave; though he recognized that this impression was helped by the thinness of her cheeks and the firmer lines that had begun to show about her mouth.

He's going to stay right here. Go on and tell what the private thing is. I can't stay all night."

He took a couple of turns up and down the floor, and then he begun, really begun this time.

"Eureka," he says, "you've been advertising for a wife—not for yourself; course I don't mean that. Ha! ha! No, I don't mean that. But you've been advertising for a wife for your Mr. Hopper man. You have, ain't you?"

At the mention of these ads Eureka had stiffened up like a wooden image. Now she flew at him.

"What if I have," she says. "What business is that of yours, Nate Scudder? How did you know about it?"

"There, there, don't get mad. I see it in the papers, of course. I—I—— Say, look here; what reward is there for that wife?"

"Reward?"

"Yes, yes, reward. What will this Mr. Hopper pay for his wife, suppose a body fetched her to him? What'll he pay?"

"Pay? Nathan Scudder, what are you talking about? Do you mean to tell me that you know——"

"I don't mean to tell you nothing. I'm just asking about that reward. See here, Eureka; suppose a——a sartin party had got track of that wife;

CONGRESSMAN PUMPHREY

soldier; in the second place, you are from a farming community and from the state where the home is located. Consequently, there will be no reason to suspect—that is, the whole thing will be quite natural."

I don't know what I said, and the next thing I knew the senator was saying good night.

"I'll send a copy of the bill around to-morrow. And we'll have some more poker in a day or two." And with that he was gone.

I didn't sleep a wink all night. To-day I went to see Mrs. Hawkesworth, but they said she was out. I haven't found her at home since the statehood bill was settled, although I've called there a number of times. I wanted to ask her advice. I can't refuse Octopus, although it will be politi-

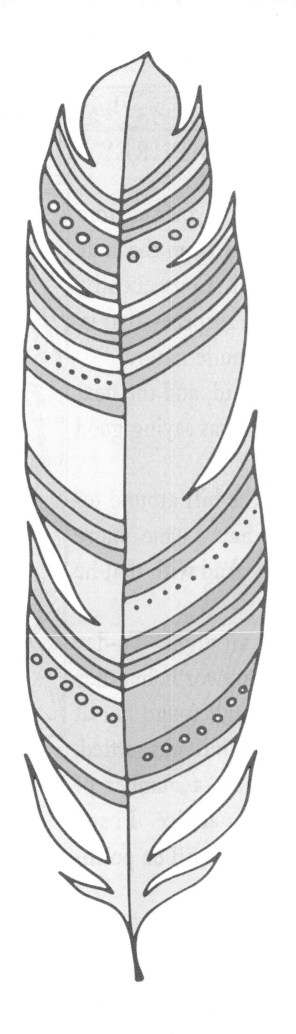

Hearts and Masks

"What a horrible night! It will haunt me as long as I live!"

I said nothing; and we did not speak again till the first of the Blankshire lights flashed by us. By this time her sobs had ceased.

"I know *I* haven't done anything especially gallant to-night; no fighting, no rescuing, and all that. They just moved *me* around like a piece of stage scenery."

A smile flashed and was gone. It was a hopeful sign.

"But the results are the same. You have admitted to me that you are neither engaged nor married. Won't you take me on—on approval?"

"Mr. Comstalk, it all seems so like a horrid dream. You *are* a brave man, and what is better, a sensible one, for you submitted to the inevitable with the best possible grace. But you talk of

advance what you would ask of me,—that your son should be rich, is it not? For this, what need have you of my aid? Make him a merchant, and let him steal like old Mansour; make him a pacha, and let him pillage his brethren; make him a dervish, and let him flatter and lie. All the vices lead to fortune when they are joined with the vilest of all,—avarice. This is the secret of life. Adieu."

"This is not what I wish," said the astonished Halima; "you do wrong to deride me in this way. My son will be an honest man like his father; and what I wish is that he may be happy here on earth."

"Virtuous and happy!" cried the dervish, with a sardonic laugh; "and you address yourself to me! My good woman, what you want is the four-leaved shamrock, which none has seen since Adam. Let your son seek it; if he finds it, be sure that he will lack for nothing."

"What is the four-leaved shamrock?" cried the anxious mother; but the magician had disappeared, never more to return. Man or demon, none has since beheld him. Halima, full of emotion, bent over the cradle and gazed at her son, who seemed to smile on her in his sleep. "Rest in peace," said she, "and rely on my love. I know not what this talisman is of which the dervish speaks, but child of my soul! we will seek it together, and something tells me that you will find it. Satan is cunning and man is weak, but God rules the heart of his faithful, and does what he will."

mysterious whisper so characteristic of him, " show us how simple and childlike is the faith of these people? They confidently expect that those bags, at the sound of Gabriel's trump, will be changed into a throng of monks — that, in the twinkling of an eye, the entire roster of the monastery, from its foundation, will stand together in a company, ready to answer the roll-call."

" I'd like to see those bags," repeated Walter.

McKenzie talked again with Brother Manoles, and reported:

" They regard this as a holy place, and do not open it to satisfy mere curiosity. Then, too, they feel that it would be disrespect to their dead brethren should they allow strangers to peer in at their bones."

" Oh, I see," replied Walter. " Well, 'tis a very natural feeling, and I respect them for it. Just the same, I have an overpowering curiosity to take a peep at those bags piled away in there, those exhibits filed for future reference. If I could get hold of the key, I'd come down here some night and steal a look at them. That would be something to tell the folks at home!"

But McKenzie was anxious to get back to his yellow book, so, after tasting the wine in several

my husband's death. I only presume to offer myself, sir," she went on, turning toward the doctor, and becoming more earnest and self-possessed in her manner as she did so—"I only presume to offer myself, with my mistress's permission, as a substitute for a nurse until some better qualified person can be found."

"What do you say, Mr. Orridge?" asked Mrs. Norbury.

It had been the doctor's turn to start when he first heard Mrs. Jazeph propose herself for the office of nurse. He hesitated before he answered Mrs. Norbury's question, then said:

"I can have but one doubt about the propriety of thankfully accepting Mrs. Jazeph's offer."

Mrs. Jazeph's timid eyes looked anxiously and perplexedly at him as he spoke. Mrs. Norbury, in her downright, abrupt way, asked immediately what the doubt was.

"I feel some uncertainty," replied Mr. Orridge, "as to whether Mrs. Jazeph—she will pardon me, as a medical man, for mentioning it—as to whether Mrs. Jazeph is strong enough, and has her nerves sufficiently under control, to perform the duties which she is so kindly ready to undertake."

In spite of the politeness of the explanation, Mrs. Jazeph was evidently disconcerted and distressed by it. A certain quiet, uncomplaining sadness, which it was very touching to see, overspread her face as she turned away, without another word, and walked slowly to the door.

"Don't go yet!" cried Mrs. Norbury, kindly,

And well he might! The situation was astounding!

Here was this young girl, Gloria de la Vera, the daintiest beauty, the wealthiest heiress in the country, proposing to marry HIM, the poor young fisherman attached to the estate! It was wonderful, unprecedented, incredible!

Why, half the young men in the community were mad to get her. A smile of hers would have brought the best of them to her feet.

And yet she came to give her hand and her fortune to this poor, unlearned young fisherman!

"Nothing, nothing but temporary insanity could have betrayed her into such a reckless proposal," said the young fisherman to himself.

Yet the girl who stood there before him, calm, pale, and steadfast as a marble statue, was not insane—no, nor immodest, nor unmaidenly, however appearances might tell against her.

Neither had she done any wrong, or even suffered any wrong; for she had scarcely a fault in her nature to lead her into any evil, and never an enemy in the world to do her any injury.

Nor had she quarreled with a betrothed lover and sought to revenge herself upon him by rushing into this low marriage; but she had never been in love and never been engaged.

Neither did she hurry towards matrimony as a refuge from domestic despotism, for she was the petted darling of a widowed and childless uncle, who had been a father to her orphanage; and she had had her own right royal will and way all her little life.

If there were any despotic tyrant at old Promontory Hall, that tyrant was the dainty little beauty,

you have made a mistake that ought to be set right."

"Why doesn't he come out with the truth?"

"The whole thing is secret."

"Why?"

Natalie shrugged hopelessly, and Gordon lost himself in frowning thought.

"This is amazing," he said, brusquely, after a moment. "It's vital. It affects all my plans. I must know everything at once."

"I'm sorry I paid so little attention."

"Never mind; try it again and be diplomatic. If O'Neil won't tell you, question Appleton—you can wind him around your fingers easily enough."

The girl eyed him with a quick change of expression.

"Isn't it enough to know that the Trust has nothing to do with the S. R. & N.?"

"No!" he declared, impatiently. "I must know the whole inside of this secret understanding—this blackmail, or whatever it is."

"Then—I'm sorry."

"Come! Don't be silly. You can do me a great service."

"You said you no longer disliked Mr. O'Neil and that he couldn't harm you."

"Well, well! Must I explain the whys and wherefores of every move I make?"

"It would be spying if I went back. The matter is confidential—I know that."

"Will you do as I ask?" he demanded.

Natalie answered him firmly: "No! I told you what I did tell only so that you might correct—"

"You rebel, eh?" Gordon spoke out furiously.

DINNER IS SERVED

Mrs. Chadwick's, and I don't know what the girl's represented, not having been there with my discerning eyes.

Once the American countess raised her lorgnette and murmured: "What a handsome butler!"

Karloff, who sat next to her, twisted his mustache and shrugged. He had seen handsome peasants before. They did not interest him. He glanced across the table at the girl, and was much annoyed that she, too, was gazing at the butler, who had successfully completed the distribution of the soup and who now stood with folded arms by the sideboard. (How I should have liked to see him!)

When the butler took away the soup-plates, Colonel Raleigh turned to his host.

"George, where the deuce did you pick up that butler?"

Annesley looked vaguely across the table at his old comrade. He had been far away in thought. He had eaten nothing.

"What?" he asked.

"I asked you where the deuce you got that butler of yours."

"Oh, Betty found him somewhere. Our own

A Crazy Angel

I've told you, have n't I, that Rev. Mr. Howard is the sort of person who is always looking out for others and neglecting himself? He's been recently interested in getting a crippled young German out of a hospital and back to his mother on the Rhine. The poor fellow seemed dying with home-sickness. I suspect that Mr. Howard paid his passage. But the day that he saw the poor lad off he got soaking wet, and the first I knew he was at the point of death with pneumonia. He thought that he was going to die, and he entrusted to me his last messages and a few simple bequests,—so pathetic, Elvira; and the sort of things that a man who's been raised in New England could never bring himself to say unless he was on what he believed to be his death-bed.

It makes me blush to think that I received his confidences under mistaken impressions,—for Doctor Percy has pulled him through. And now the most patient, the most grateful, and the least calculated to take care of himself—that's the sort of convalescent he makes.

Yet, I'm glad to say, he's not a saint. A "white devil," as John Bunyan puts it, has shown itself when Miss Cholmondeley's companionship has been offered for an afternoon. He said that to watch her making an antimacassar would bring on a relapse. "Her gentility," he said, very fierce, like a child who knows he's naughty, "is like the air in some musty old crypt." Did you ever hear the like? And him just out of the jaws of death.

"And," he went on, "I won't take that

The two younger Bobbsey twins felt sorry that their father had to go away, but they were told he would soon be back again. But as Flossie and Freddie were having such fun playing with Laddie, they did not really think much about Mr. Bobbsey going away, except for five minutes or so.

"Give our love to Uncle Jack," said Freddie, as he kissed his father, and started back for the Whipple rooms, where he and Laddie were building a bridge of books for the toy train of cars to cross a river, which was made of a piece of broken looking glass.

"And here's an extra kiss I'll give you for him," said Flossie, as she hugged her father in bidding him good-bye. "I love Uncle Jack."

So Mr. Bobbsey went back to Lakeport, and Mrs. Bobbsey got ready to take Nan and Bert to the Natural History Museum. At first it had been planned to take Flossie and Freddie, but, as they said they did not care much about stuffed animals, and as they were having such fun with Laddie, Mrs. Whipple told Mrs. Bobbsey she would look after the smaller twins and give them their lunch.

CHAPTER XIII

HOGARTH stared ahead at the sharp outline of the island. How strangely unchanged it appeared; how, somehow, silently eternal! He only was fluid; it was static. Twelve years had left no perceptible mark upon it; perhaps even twelve centuries had not changed it materially; yet he—he drew in his breath with sharp pain, almost fear—he was an old man, at least in comparison with the enthusiastic, carefree, happy young fellow who had first gone there twenty years before.

He had arrived in Naples early that morning, coming by the Southern route. Ischia had risen out of the mist to greet him; then Capri, on the right, an unfamiliar outline to him as seen from the sea; then small islands, the precipitous point of Posillipo, and at last smiling Naples and brooding Vesuvius. Noisy fruit vendors in row boats, naked boys diving for coins, vociferous coachmen and guides, bored custom officials, vast cheerless chambers of the Custom House filled with complaining, impatient travelers, and finally—blazing sunlight and the familiar, pungent, unescapable scent of Naples. Antonia had once said that the smell of Naples was its most personal characteristic, a passionate blending of the scent of goats, oranges and incense. She had laughingly admitted she adored it.

Antonia!

Hogarth threw himself down on the seat of the

PETER LAYS A PLOT

val before he was called for supper to the other house. She seemed to have recovered entirely from her indisposition and was intensely, almost hilariously, gay. Her cheeks were bright with color and her eyes sparkled with animation as she talked.

Varenka Petrovna, on the contrary, was silent and depressed, and when her eyes met her father's, they turned aside with the frightened look which they had shown when she became conscious that he had been a witness to her indiscretion with Ivan Egorovitch earlier in the day. Had she been less reticent and absorbed, it is probable that Motrya Petrovna would have let out to her her secret, for her heart was so full of it that it trembled constantly on her tongue. But the older sister shrank from an exchange of confidences and kept her husband by her so that no chance of them should occur.

When Peter Efimovitch returned from his meal, Ossip Pavelovitch and his wife were busy in the house and Motrya Petrovna sat by herself in the dusk, on a bench, outside the door. He seated himself absently beside her and, taking out his pipe, filled it and settled himself to smoke.

The girl smiled up at him affectionately as he

THE CHARLATANS

"B-r-a-h-m-s." Mrs. Maybury spelled out the strange word, smiling. "I am especially interested in Brahms. I will play his Second Rhapsody."

Hope's first sensation was one of bewilderment. Her ear was unprepared for the strange harmonies that poured tumultuously upon it. This sensation gave way to a physical tremulousness, and tears started in her eyes. Unaware of the effect she was producing, the pianist began the climax of the Rhapsody, and the fierce rush of it swept Hope into hysteria. She felt she must cry out, beseech the lady to stop playing, or fly the room. She rose, but dizziness took her, and she sank back again. She was sobbing when the music ceased.

Surprised and pleased, Mrs. Maybury put an arm about the neophyte's shoulders. "Dear girl," she said, "I have never had so sympathetic a listener."

She played for an hour or more, until she came to the end of her repertory, which, she remarked, was brief in summer. . . .

The promised books came promptly: a volume of Czerny studies, Bach's Inventions, and the first volume of Beethoven's Sonatas.

"When you can play Czerny up to tempo," wrote Enlightenment, "you can play anything. But Bach!

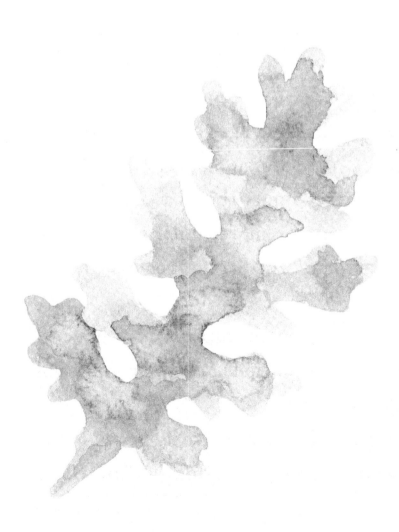

unaccountable influence over him as, sleeping or waking, to be ever present in his thoughts. After another furtive look around, to make sure no one present but himself was in possession of the knowledge that the Rev. Horace Harding was sore hit in the dangerous region of the heart, he settled down to listen.

The speaker was saying, "I know a woman who left a home of luxury for one which proved to be the home of a drunkard. Her husband was a lawyer, and used his position and influence and vote against the cause of prohibition. He died in poverty. His widow wrought as best she could, with untrained hands, to educate her boy and save her little home from the governmental tax hammer. She succeeded. To-day her boy drinks and votes. She pays the taxes and weeps.

"The government, in the press and on the hustings, vociferates, 'I am of the people, for the people, by the people.' It is a false statement. Our government is not as representative as it gives itself credit for being. Man fought for his vantage ground and gained it inch by inch. If by the accident of birth he found himself a son of poverty in days that are gone, he was excluded from privileges he now justly claims are but his due. However, forgetting his past, he now

went to sleep. Then Oh again tied him to the wood, and burned him, and scattered the ashes to the four winds, and sprinkled the remnant of the coal with living water, and instead of the loutish clown there stood there such a handsome and stalwart Cossack* that the like of him can neither be imagined nor described, but only told of in tales.

There, then, the lad remained for a year, and at the end of the year the father came for his son. He came to the self-same charred stumps in the self-same forest, sat him down, and said:

"Oh!"

Oh immediately came out of the charred stump, and said:

"Hail! O man!"

"Hail to thee, Oh!"

"And what dost thou want, O man?" asked Oh.

"I have come," said he, "for my son."

"Well, come, then! If thou dost know

---

* *Kozak*, a Cossack, being the ideal human hero of the Ruthenians; just as a *bogatry* is a hero of the demi-god type, as the name implies.

at the foot of the town; and Spiro himself, landing with impatient haste, climbed the winding path and flung across the square to the missionary's house. The tassel of his fez danced merrily as he walked, and his cheeks were as brown as a nut from the kiss of the winds of the sea. Straight to the missionary's front door he went and knocked loudly. It was Polyxene who opened for him, and he greeted her with a glad cry and a movement as though he would push in and take her in his arms. But she thrust out her arm and said:

"Sh! Mr. Ion is very sick. Did you wish to see me, Spiro?" For she had no mind to avoid an interview, but rather to suggest one and have the matter settled as soon as possible.

"Did I wish to see you?" he laughed. "'Tis not strange if a man should wish to see his affianced bride, is it?"

"No, no, not at all," she replied; "but Mr. Ion is really very sick and we can not talk here. Wait for me a moment, and I will walk with you upon the beach."

Tying a handkerchief about her head, she joined him and together they walked down to the sea-shore, and strolled along the snowy sands,

FOR HER SAKE

"You must let me stay," Mildred pleaded.

"Yes — I want you to hear it out to the end; and you, too," he added, flashing a look upon George.

George made a slight movement forward so that when Barton entered the room he was confronted by their concentrated gaze. The man's appearance spoke his condition plainly; his face looked careworn, his heavily lined features giving him the appearance of dissoluteness. He stopped near the door and faced the three people, while a strange expression of uncertainty flashed across his face; then, with evident concentration, he walked resolutely towards Mr. Livingstone and held out his hand.

"We can dispense with formality, Barton," Mr. Livingstone said, withholding his hand.

Barton's look of greeting changed, and he gave George a swift look of interrogation. Receiving nothing in answer but a blank expression, he shifted his look to Mrs. Braeme and then came slowly back to Mr. Livingstone.

"I don't understand," he said finally. "I received a telephone message saying you wanted me to come here at once. Was there a mistake?"

Mr. Livingstone drew his arm from Mildred's grasp and went forward to Barton, looking him squarely in the eyes.

"Barton," he said slowly, painfully distinct, "is what this man has told me true?" He indicated George with a nod of the head.

Barton's face went ashy and his mouth trembled so that for a moment he seemed unable to speak.

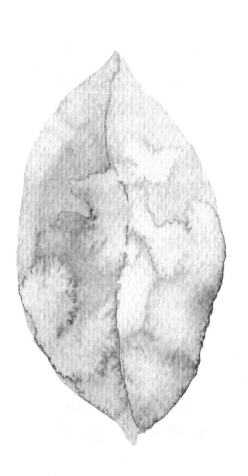

of brown or black carved woodwork, with elaborate dormers, and fine clusterings of red roofs. To any west-country Englishman these are very welcome sights.

The weather had turned, and a cool wind blew against us from the ridges; it seemed already the breath of the Atlantic seaboard. We went one day up to Coburg to fetch our letters—a self-centred, self-sufficient little place, with a huge château on the hill-top, and comfortable villas in the valley. There is a feudal gateway; also a typical old market-place, with a characterless statue of Prince Albert in the centre of it. Coburg is an epitome of German ducalism; there is just enough antiquity about it to prevent it seeming wholly artificial.

We found our way out again into Bavaria, and slept in a rural wilderness, where half-timber hamlets lie lost in the clearings of the forest. You struggle along the sandy and stony ways, and suddenly come upon a group of cottages and a grey church-spire. Surely they must have grown there, moulded by their environment, like the ragged wind-caught pines. At Ober Elldorf the inn was signless; but such sweetly primitive places are the true guest-houses. You will find no advertisement of them, even in those

"I used to dream," he said, "of you and me as wed . . in honor."

"Oh, I would wed you in dishonor, in disgrace, in death! See," she said hurriedly, "here is my mother's wedding-ring. I have always worn it about my neck. I love you! I love you!" She laid it in his hand.

"Put it upon my finger," she whispered. "Say it after me: 'I, Anne, take thee, Louis, to my wedded husband . . . '"

A strange fire had come into his face.

"'I, Louis,'" he repeated solemnly, "'take thee, Anne, to my wedded wife . . . '"

"'To have and to hold, from this day forward, for better, for worse, for richer, for poorer, in sickness and in health . . . '"

"'To have and to hold, from this day forward, for better, for worse, for richer, for poorer, in sickness and in health . . . '"

She was sobbing now so that she could scarcely frame the words:

"'To love and to cherish—till death us do—' join, Louis! It can not, it shall not part us!"

"My own love!" he said in choked tones, and held her quivering against his breast.

"The time is up," said the voice.

Anne clasped Armand with her young arms—

the sagging gate. She drew quickly back into the shadow. Then whirring in a lower key — then dead stop.

Then his darling voice saying low to Cox, "Come about eight. Tell Fow just to say I'm out of town for the night."

Then soft whirring again lost in his voice saying to Linda at the open door just below, "Of course I'm going to stay all night. Late getting away from the hospital. Always wanted to sleep out here in the Gloucester hammock under the pines. Fearfully hot in town. You must get some rest. Miss Frame here?"

"Thank God, yes! Such a comfort to have her. She's a dear!"

"She's got courage — lots of it. Lean on her. Now you rest. Take two of the white tablets I gave you — and sleep. Don't give me a thought — unless you need me."

"Oh, you good man! You good, good man!"

Then a silence till the hammock creaked out under the pines.

Georgia leaned far out again, listening for his breathing. Her cheeks glowed in spite of the wind that blew cool up from the thickets of wild grape. A light in the old gray farmhouse, off to the east, went out.

But it was not until the sky changed, and the whole world twittered and fluted with bird notes, that she let herself go down to waken him. And he,

conclusion, "I am agitated a little perhaps, but I am not hurt, and am ready to go to the fair. Send for To-ga-to-maugh, and let us be off while we have a chance to obtain seats in the cars, which later in the day usually are filled to overflowing long before they reach this point from the central part of the city."

I accepted his statement with a reservation; and soon after our arrival in the grounds, I was satisfied, from a persistent flush in his face and a tremulous uncertainty in his movements, that he had been affected by the fall more seriously than he imagined, or confessed; and distressing visions of the awful fate of my father, as the result of his fall, began to rise before me and blind me to everything in the world save the all-involving significance of the visible figure of my afflicted husband at my side.

Procuring a rolling-chair, I prevailed on him by a little pardonable wile, to sit in it and be wheeled to the lake-side of the grounds, where a refreshing breeze was coming in over the vast expanse of Lake Michigan, and where I could get for him a cup of his favorite Cingalese tea, and test for myself the extent of his injuries by the reaction effected in him by the most favorable circumstances.

And here we had our luncheon in due time and remained until three o'clock in the afternoon, when we went leisurely to the southwestern corner of the Court of Honor, where, in the latter part of the afternoon, when the effects of sunshine and shadow are the most effective from an artistic point of view, I usually made it a point to go to behold as a whole with ineffable rapture, and to study in detail with infinite delight, the most magnificent and beautiful expression of the genius of Man in an objective structural form the world has ever seen.

Having arrived at my favorite point of view, To-ga-to-maugh took a seat a little distance from us, and I took his place at the back of the rolling-chair in which Philemon sat in an unusual silence and indifference, with respect to his unseen situation and surroundings and my actions and thoughts, which I attributed to his accident in the morning. Presently, while I was looking over his hat and dreamily wandering in mind across the sheen of the Grand Basin, past the glittering statue of the Republic, and through the central arch of the superb Eastern Peristyle, and losing myself along the indistinct line where the curve of Lake Michigan interblended with the overarching azure of infinity, I was recalled suddenly and tumultuously, and with a perceptible shudder coursing through my body, by Philemon addressing me in a tone of independence and self-assertion I had not heard him utter since our last happy meeting and parting before the destruction of Johnstown.

toward the River; then he turned away and disappeared on the Desert.

"Slippery looked worried," commented Johnny, when they could no longer distinguish his gray form among the brush. "You may be sure he is trying to keep out of the way of some one he is afraid of. Now, who can it be?"

As the hours passed, and no one else came near that pile of stones, Johnny grew bold enough to climb up on the Ridge to a low point, where a twisted old mesquite tree had tried for years to grow in the scanty soil between the rocks. There Johnny sat and nibbled the dry mesquite beans, and watched a beautiful Bluebird flit

"I knew," he said, "that you wanted to come and sit on my knee!"

"I never did," replied Winsome with animation, making a statement almost certainly inaccurate upon the face of it.

"That's why you sent away the children," he went on, pinching her ear.

"Of all things in this world," said Winsome indignantly, "commend me to a man for conceit!"

"And to winsome wives for wily ways!" said her husband instantly. To do him justice, he did not often do this sort of thing.

"Keep the alliteration for the poems," retorted Winsome. "Truth will do for me."

After a little while she said, without apparent connection:

"It is very hot."

"What are they doing in the hay-field?" asked Ralph.

"Jock Forrest was leading and they were cutting down the croft very steadily. I think it looks like sixty bushels to the acre," she continued practically; "so you shall have a carpet for the study this year, if all goes well."

"That will be famous!" cried Ralph, like a schoolboy, waving his hand. It paused among Winsome's hair.

"I wish you would not tumble it all down," she said; "I am too old for that kind of thing now!"

The number of times good women perjure themselves is almost unbelievable.

But the recording angel has, it is said, a deaf side, otherwise he would need an ink-eraser. Ralph knew very well what she really meant, and continued to throw the fine-spun glossy waves over her head, as a miser may toss his gold for the pleasure of the cool, crisp touch.

"Then," continued Winsome, without moving (for, though so unhappy and uncomfortable, she sat still—some

A Lesson in Fiction

lunge (one he had learnt at home out of a book of lunges) and——

Very good. You have answered correctly. Now, suppose you find, a little later in the book, that the killing of Hairy Hank has compelled De Vaux to flee from his native land to the East. Are you not fearful for his safety in the desert?

Answer. Frankly, I am not. De Vaux is all right. His name is on the title page, and you can't kill him.

Question. Listen to this, then: "The sun of Ethiopia beat fiercely upon the desert as De Vaux, mounted upon his faithful elephant, pursued his lonely way. Seated in his lofty hoo-doo, his eye scoured the waste. Suddenly a solitary horseman appeared on the horizon, then another, and another, and then six. In a few moments a whole crowd of solitary horsemen swooped down upon him. There was a fierce shout of 'Allah!' a rattle of fire-arms. De Vaux sank from his hoo-doo on to the sands, while the affrighted elephant dashed off in all directions. The bullet had struck him in the heart."

There now, what do you think of that? Isn't De Vaux killed now?

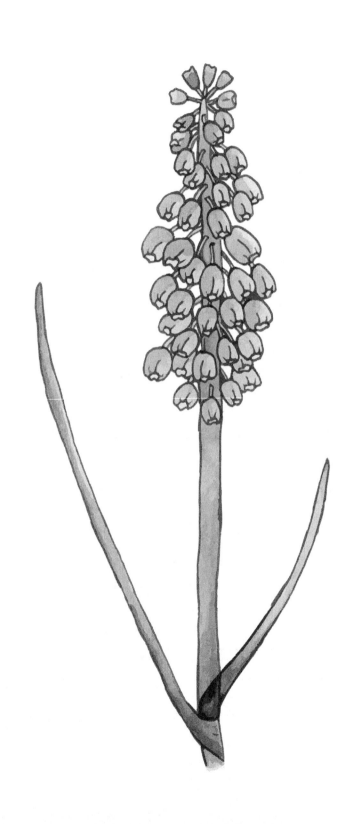

"Oh, he's always yelling for help. They've coddled him so long in the family that he acts like a ten-year-old kid. I stole a kiss from Celeste one day, and I will be shot if he didn't start to blubber."

"You stole a kiss, eh?" said James, admiringly.

"Only just for the sport of making him crazy, that was all." But William's red visage belied his indifferent tone. "You'd better go and see what he wants. My hands are all harness grease."

Warburton concluded to follow William's advice. He flung down his paper and strode out to the rear porch, where he saw Pierre gesticulating wildly.

"What's the matter? What do you want?"—churlishly.

"Frightful! Zee stove-pipe ees vat you call *bust!*"

James laughed.

"I can not rrreach eet. I can not cook till eet ees fix'. You are tall, eh?"—affably.

"All right; I'll help you fix it."

Grumbling, James went into the kitchen, mounted a chair, and began banging away at the

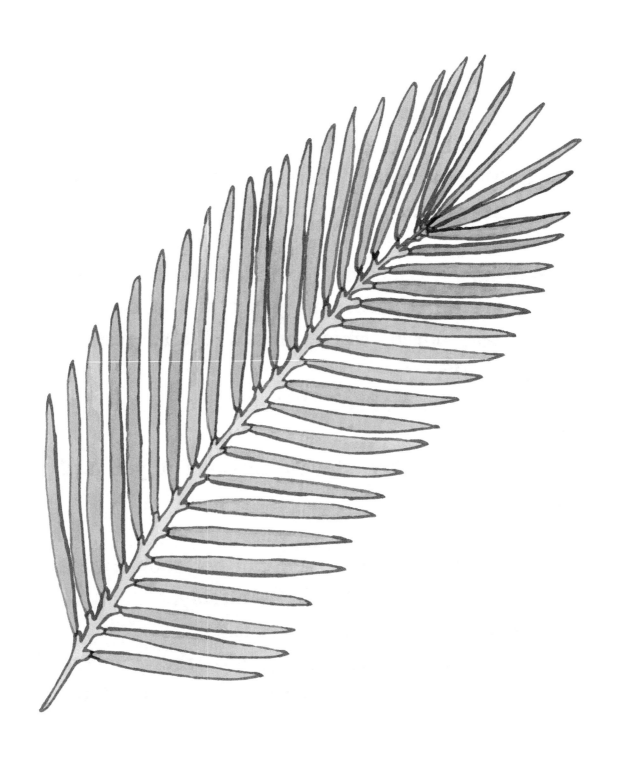

country, back to town, off for the railway yard and back to Cahill's. He was only eighteen. How was he to know that the men had set a trap for him and he had walked feverishly into it?

They kept him there at Cahill's until nine o'clock that night. Once they lost sight of him; but as he came out of the washroom, they sighed relievedly. As a matter of fact, though, he had slipped through the alley window and into the adjacent tailor-shop from where he had telephoned the office that he was trailing three German spies and wouldn't report for his assignment.

And what did they do in the *Herald* office? Laughed. Why not? It was only the cub, off on one of his wild-goose chases.

At nine the men departed, and the cub began his trailing again. This time there were no tortuous windings. The men headed directly toward the railway yard, and the cub decided that they were going to wreck the Mansfield steel mills.

There was a deal of freight movement. Nighttime there generally is. And there were many broken strings of empties to cut across. Once he regretted he hadn't asked for a partner in this enterprise.

Suddenly his men vanished. The boy fell into a dog-trot to the end of a string of empties. As he passed the last car, the sky fell out. When he

pression of the room in which she had immured her darling had infected the sunny air of this glorious day and made free breathing an impossibility. The weights on her feet were so palpable to her that she unconsciously looked down at them. This was how she came to notice the dust on her shoes. Alive to the story it told, she burst the spell which held her and made a bound toward the house.

Rushing to her room she shook her skirts and changed her shoes, and thus freed from all connecting links with that secret spot, reentered among her guests, as beautiful and probably as wretched a woman as the world contained that day.

Yet not as wretched as she could be. There were depths beneath these depths. If he should ever know! If he should ever come to look at her with horrified, even alienated eyes! Ah, that were the end—that would mean the river for her—the river which all were so soon to think had swallowed the little Gwendolen. Was that Miss Graham coming? Was the stir she now heard outside, the first indication of the hue and cry which would soon ring through the whole place and her shrinking heart

JOHN'S VICTORY

He turned over some books on the table.

"I want to confide to you," he went on, "that in the autumn I intend to enter upon another large—if not larger—field. I mean to write a contemplative study of the lives of the early bishops. My former labor has qualified me for the chronicling of this peculiar era. But, during the summer, I wish to do some light form of literary work. And I think I have almost decided what it is to be."

Leonida freed her branch of roses and roused herself. "Yes?"

"Yes, I have almost decided. My knowledge of the German language is far from superficial, and I think I shall translate into it some of the Welsh legends in your little book there." He pointed to a little volume on the table before him. "You read aloud to me, if you remember, one night when I could not sleep, one especially charming little tale. It greatly impressed me. There are many ways in which you can help me, Leonida. To begin with, I shall ask you often to read the English

THE SPLIT

One of the first startlers she landed in Carthage was a letter in which she said:

Just time for a line, mother honey. I'm so dog tired of nights I fall asleep in the midst of my prayers, if I remember to say them at all—which is not always. I poured 2,640 cups of chocolate to-day—which is going some for little Edna, as the boys call me.

Thank the Lord, to-night I shall sleep in sheets for the first time in a month. We don't get them, but the nicest young sergeant you ever saw got a pair issued to him, and he said he couldn't bear to use them when I had none, so he gave them to me.

Don't be excited, mother darling; he's perfectly nice. He's an American sergeant sent ahead on some *liaison* work for the Intelligence. He only gave me the sheets because I had lent him my hot-water bottle one night when he had cramps in his tummie. So you see it's perfectly all right.

Now I'm off to dreamland's ice-creamy mountains until, as the song says, "that dirty pup wakes the bugler up."

Poor Mrs. Eby was still quivering with this when Edna's next letter announced the approach of a certain Lady Keenbrook.

We're all crazy to see what she looks like. We've never seen a real lady with a capital L.

Belle Cumbers says that she intends to show this English snob that an American lady is quite as good as anybody, but it's easy to see that Belladonna (as we call her, because she makes such eyes at the men) is simply perishing to rub up against her. So are we all.

Nighty-night, mother dear. I'm so proud I don't know what to do. I broke the record in cigarette sales to-day. I sold more Bill Durhams, Fat Emmas, and Sweet Caps than anybody ever sold before at this canteen.

The sergeant I spoke to you about tried to teach me to "roll my own," as he so cutely phrased it. When I told him I had never smoked, he wouldn't believe me. He said that such ignorance was pitiful, and I suppose it is, but there is a strict rule that forbids us poor Red Triangleines to smoke, so I shall have to wait till this cruel war is over.

MORE BLACKOUT POETRY JOURNALS

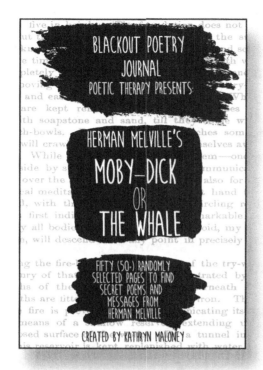

AVAILABLE ON AMAZON NOW

Bonus Page from Kathryn's next blackout poetry journals curently in progress.

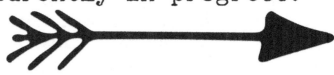

She looked down at his thick, wavy, black hair. 'What a wreck of a bad man,' she thought, almost regretfully. Yet he was young enough as far as years went. Not yet thirty. About ten years her senior. It was ridiculous at barely twenty to have lived through all her experiences. It seemed such an age since her mother had brought her to Paris, a shy little girl of twelve. Two years later

"You might have kissed me," he sobbed. "If you had kissed me I would have understood. We are strangers to each other." She kept her temper admirably. "What babies men are!" she said gaily. She held up her face. "I am waiting." He bowed stiffly. "Not now. I am not yet a beggar." He flung himself down on a sofa by the window. A shaft of sunshine touched his face. Involuntarily Therzia noticed how pimpled and blotchy his skin looked. He was not properly shaved either. His eyes had a furtive, frightened look and his big, loose lips were suspiciously red. She passed her fingers over her own mouth. Did he use some pigment? Or was it only fever? No wonder the poor man did not sleep well at nights. And his bed-room was so luxurious! She turned round, pushed her chair forward, and looked

"I had nothing to bring, but a hungry man's excellent appetite." (He had eaten nothing all day.) From the adjoining saloon, through the murmur of general conversation, came the sound of a woman's light laughter. It rang like a bell, clear and joyous, evidently dominating the situation. M.Bourrienne's guests were amusing themselves, Bonaparte felt himself an interloper. What had he to do with a pack of pleasure-seekers? He drew his brows together — moody, silent, miserable. Peter beckoned to the footman. "You are wanted In the dining-room," he said. "Here, take these parcels. Dish them and place them on the table. Scraps!" he muttered beneath

What Women Meme
The journal for women's thoughts.

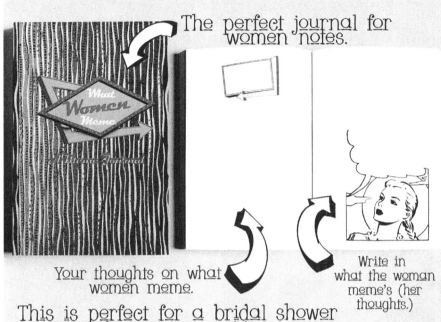

The perfect journal for women notes.

Your thoughts on what women meme.

Write in what the woman meme's (her thoughts.)

This is perfect for a bridal shower with everyone adding their thoughts and wishes.

"Oh, that's all over," said Jane. "You're off the bed-plane now, and don't you see how much higher you've got already? The next step is to fix yourself so securely on this happy one that you know that it's yours and you can't leave it. You see, you feel able to go back down again, and as long as you feel that way, it's possible. One has to bar out the wrong kind of life forever, and then of course it's over." "But she is coming back," said Susan, "and I can't live any more on gobbles of milk and cold bits swallowed while I'm getting up-stairs three steps to the jump." Jane looked at her. "I expect that exercise was awfully good for you, Auntie," she said seriously. "You've probably gotten a lot of health and interest out of it. Don't forget that." "Well, maybe; but I don't want any more." Susan's tone was terribly earnest. "It's all over then," said Jane, slowly and with emphasis; "if you truly and honestly don't want any more, then it must be all over. The thing to do now is to build a firm connection between ourselves and it's being all over."

"I don't quite understand what you mean," said Susan, "but something's got to be done, of course, because otherwise she'll come home, and oh, my, her face when she sees me up and around!"

Jane knit her brows, ... "You see, Auntie," she said slowly, "there's only one thing to do. We've got to change ourselves completely; we've to get where we want her to come home and where we look forward to it—" Susan stopped short and lifted up both hands. "Gracious, we can't ever do that! It isn't in humanity." "Yes, we can do it," said Jane firmly; "people can always do anything that they can think out, and if we can think this out straight, we can do it." "How?" "It isn't easy to see in just the first minute, but I understand the principle of it and I know that we can work it, for I've seen it done. You do it by getting an entirely new atmosphere into

REDACTED NAVY JOURNAL

Rewriting (redacting) NAVY manual narratives to make them better.

← you redact the pages like an expert!

There is always more than one version of offical publications - your version!

Kathryn I Maloney

AVIATION SUPPLY
NAVY TRAINING: 1945

How to read and add to this journal.

Clip, redact, and glue your article on this side.

You redact the manual on this side.
only a sample

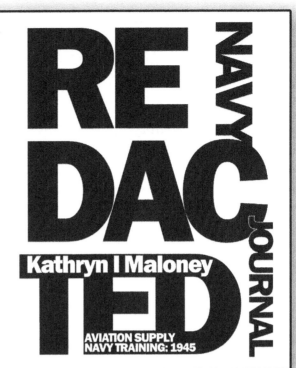

Get started ⇨

2017 (c) kimaloney
www.kimaloney.com

YOU CAN HELP

This may be a relief to you. Every Table of Basic Allowances carries with it full instructions on its use—what the columns are, which ones are guides only and which must be followed to the letter. And remember, too, that although the best minds of ASO, BuAer, BuOrd and even British aeronautical engineering are thrown together to produce the tables, admittedly they aren't perfect products.

Each of the bureaus or agencies producing them wants suggestions from YOU, any time you notice where the allowances seem out of order. You're in the field and are in a good position to keep the technicians at home fully advised of conditions as they develop regarding Aviation Supply.

Figure 11.—Your suggestions are needed.

No end of time has been saved in the past by these Tables of Basic Allowances when an activity was about to be commissioned and when the period for replenishment of supplies came around. They've served well

Made in the USA
Monee, IL
11 February 2023